NEW

The paper boy
and other stories

Nelson

Not at the party

Yin-May had spots.
She had spots on her face and
spots on her neck and
spots on her arms.
She had to stay in bed.

Mum said to Emma,

Yin-May can't come to your party.

Emma was sad.

Can I write a letter to Yin-May?

said Emma.

Mum gave her a sheet of paper.

Emma wrote a letter to Yin-May.

3

This is what Emma wrote.

I am sorry you can't come
to my party.
Look out of your window
today at six o'clock.
Have a long bit of string
in your hand.
Love from
Emma

to
Yin May

Yin-May read the letter.
Emma is my best friend,
she said.
I wonder what the string is for.
I don't know, said Yin-May's Mum.
She found a very long bit
of string for Yin-May.

At six o'clock Yin-May
looked out of her window.
What a surprise, she said.
She saw all her friends who
had been at Emma's party.

They had balloons and party hats.
They clapped their hands and
waved when they saw
Yin-May at the window.

Let down the string Yin-May,
said Emma.
But keep one end in your hand.
So Yin-May let down the string and
Emma tied the end to a basket.
Then all her friends put a present
for Yin-May in the basket.

There were sweets and balloons and
cards and a big bit of birthday
cake from Emma.
You are a good friend, said Yin-May.
Now I can join in the party too.

The paper boy

Wake up Joe, said Mum.

It's time to get up.

Joe did not want to get out of bed.

It was warm in bed and

it was cold and dark outside.

Up you get, said Mum.

It's time you began your paper round.

So Joe had to get up.

He got his bicycle from the shed.

The man in the shop gave him

the papers and

Joe set off on his round.

Here was a sports paper.

That was for Sam's Dad.

He liked to read the football news.

This paper was for Yin-May's Mum.
Miss Finn read this paper with
lots of pictures.
The man in the big house read
this pink paper.
There was a big dog at his house
which barked at Joe and
nearly bit his leg.

Joe went on down the street.
He was looking at a comic for Tom
when a van with no lights on
backed out fast into the street.
The van just missed Joe but
it made him fall off his bicycle.
All his papers fell in the road.

The van didn't stop.

Joe's friend the postman
came to help him.

That was a near thing, he said.

Did you get his number Joe?

No I didn't, said Joe.

He picked up his papers.

I must hurry, he said.

I don't want to be late for school.

Joe put a paper in the letter box of
the last house.

Then he heard a shout.

Help. Help.

Joe looked through the letter box.

He saw an old man on the floor.

Help, said the old man.

I fell down the stairs.

Run and tell my sister.

She lives next door.

So Joe ran next door to

tell the old man's sister.

They went to the old man's house.
What a good thing you heard him,
said the old man's sister.
I think he has broken his leg.
Can you tell the doctor Joe?
Yes, said Joe.
When Joe got home at last
he was very, very late but
what a paper round it had been.

Away went the hat

Look Nick, said Sally.
I've got a paper hat.
Nick took the hat and
put it on a stick.
Give it back, said Sally.
But just then the wind blew and
away went the hat.

Sorry Sally, said Nick.

I'll get it back.

He ran after the hat and

Sally ran too.

What are you doing? said Sanjay.

We want to get Sally's hat,

said Nick.

I'll help you, said Sanjay.

The hat flew up into the sky.

The wind blew it out of the garden
and into the park.

Sally, Nick and Sanjay ran after it.

There it is by the swing,
said Sanjay.

But just then the wind blew again
and away went the hat.

Up it went high into the sky, over
the path and into a field.

Where is it now? said Sally.

Moo, said the cow. Moo. Moo.

Look, said Nick. The cow has got
your hat on.

They ran into the field.

But just as Nick got to the cow,

the wind blew again.

Away went the hat, up into the sky.

Oh dear, said Sally.

Where is it now?

Look, said Sanjay.

It's in that tree.

I can just get it.

The hat was torn and no good but

Sanjay wanted to get it for Sally.

He lifted up the hat and

what did he see?

Look Sally. Look Nick, said Sanjay.
In the tree was a little robin's
nest and inside the nest were
five little eggs.
That was a better find than
a paper hat, said Sally as
they went quietly away.